See

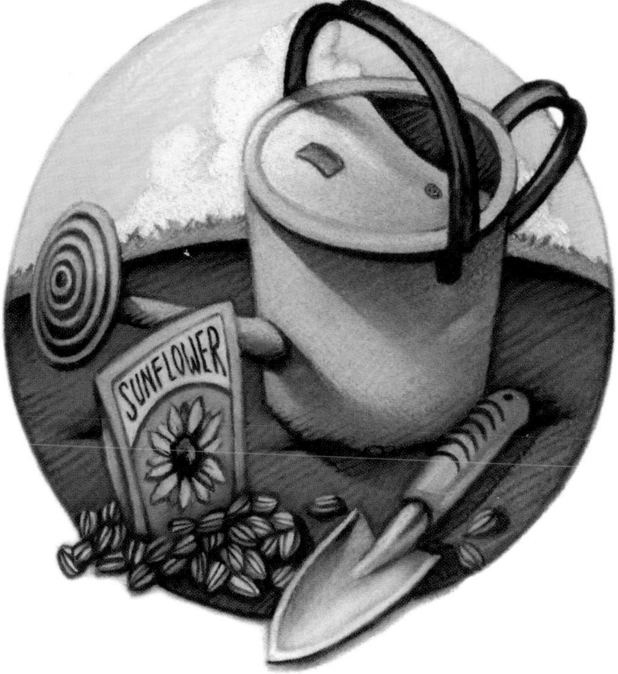

by Barbara Wood
illustrated by Doug Bowles

HAMPTON-BROWN

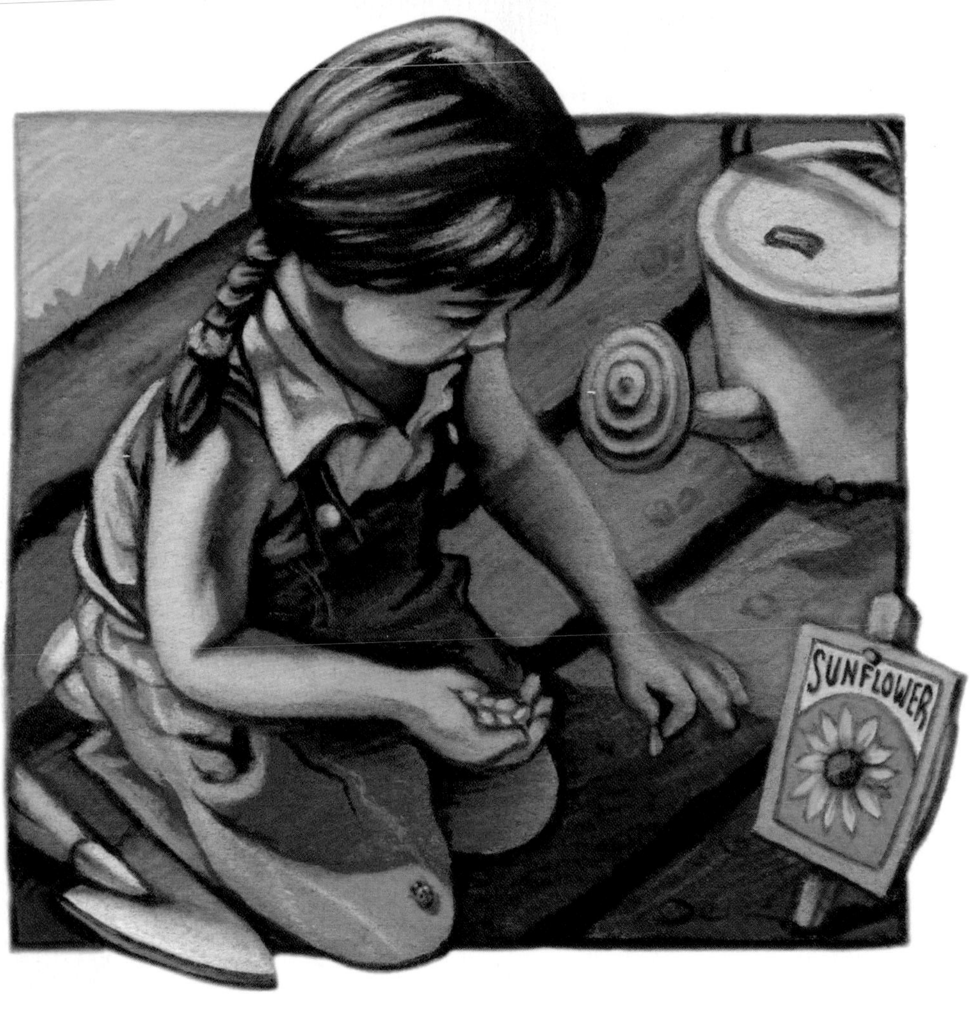

Look at the seeds.

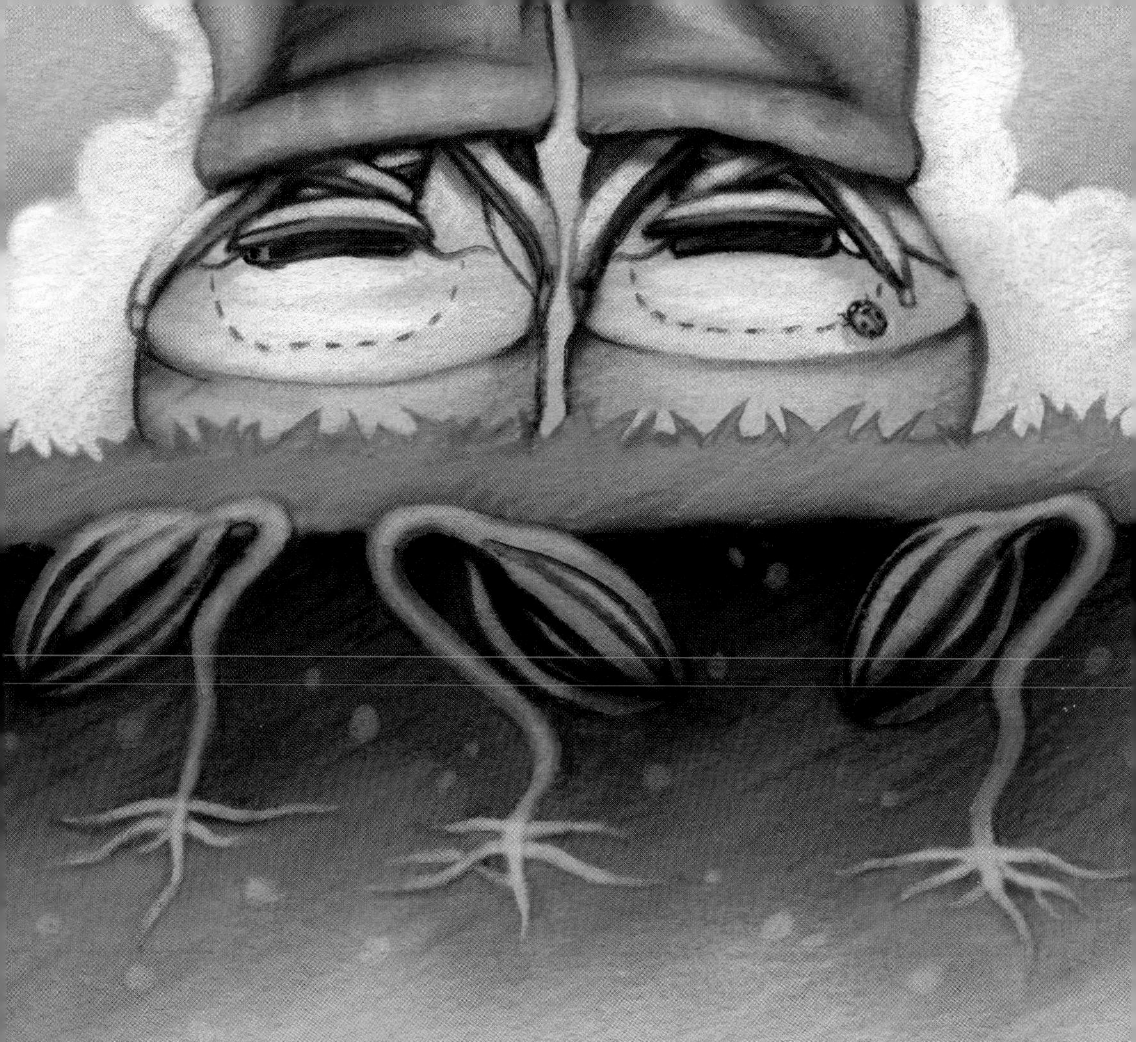

Look at the roots.

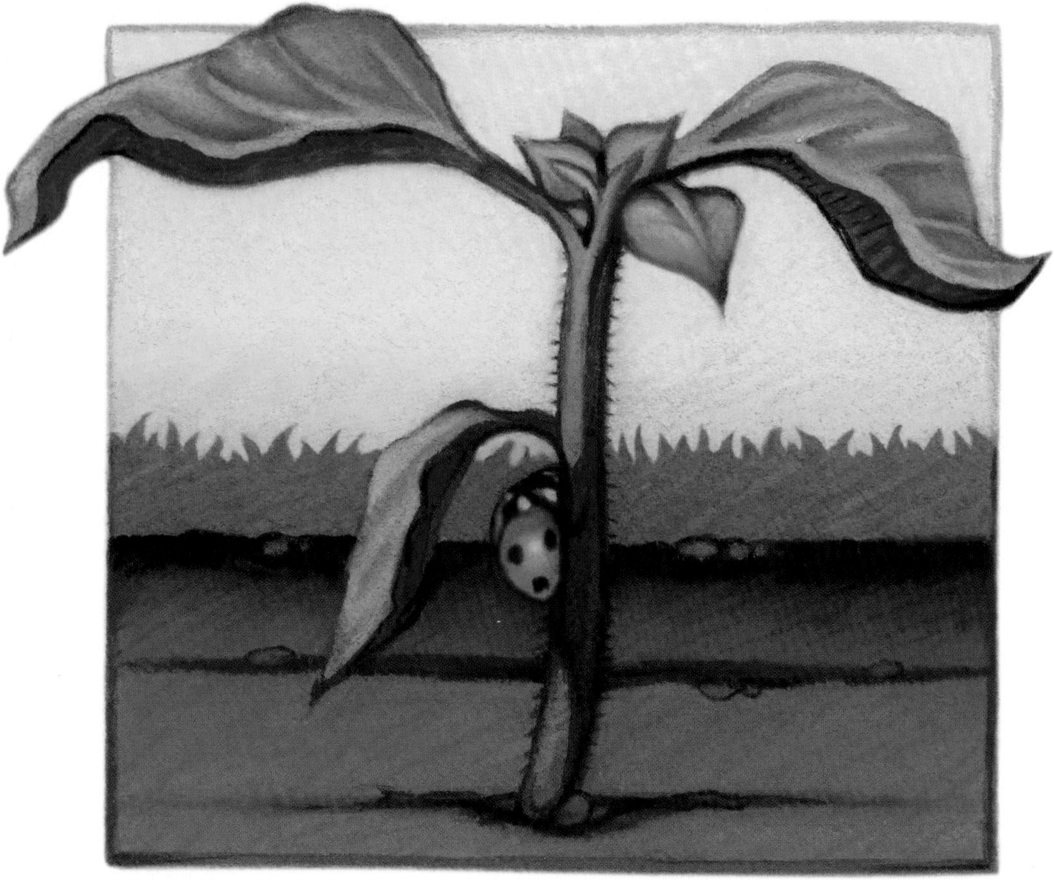

Look at the stem.

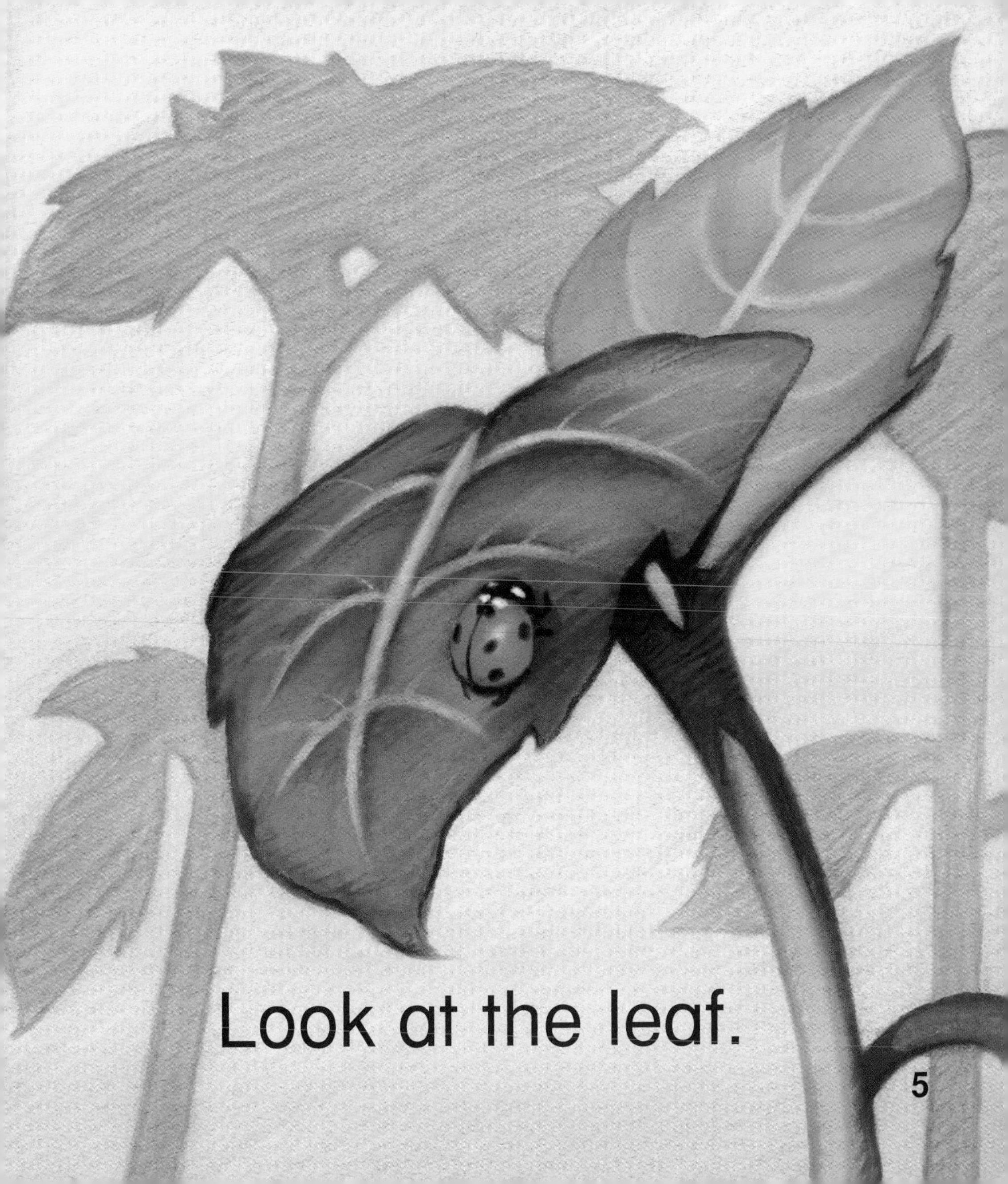

Look at the leaf.

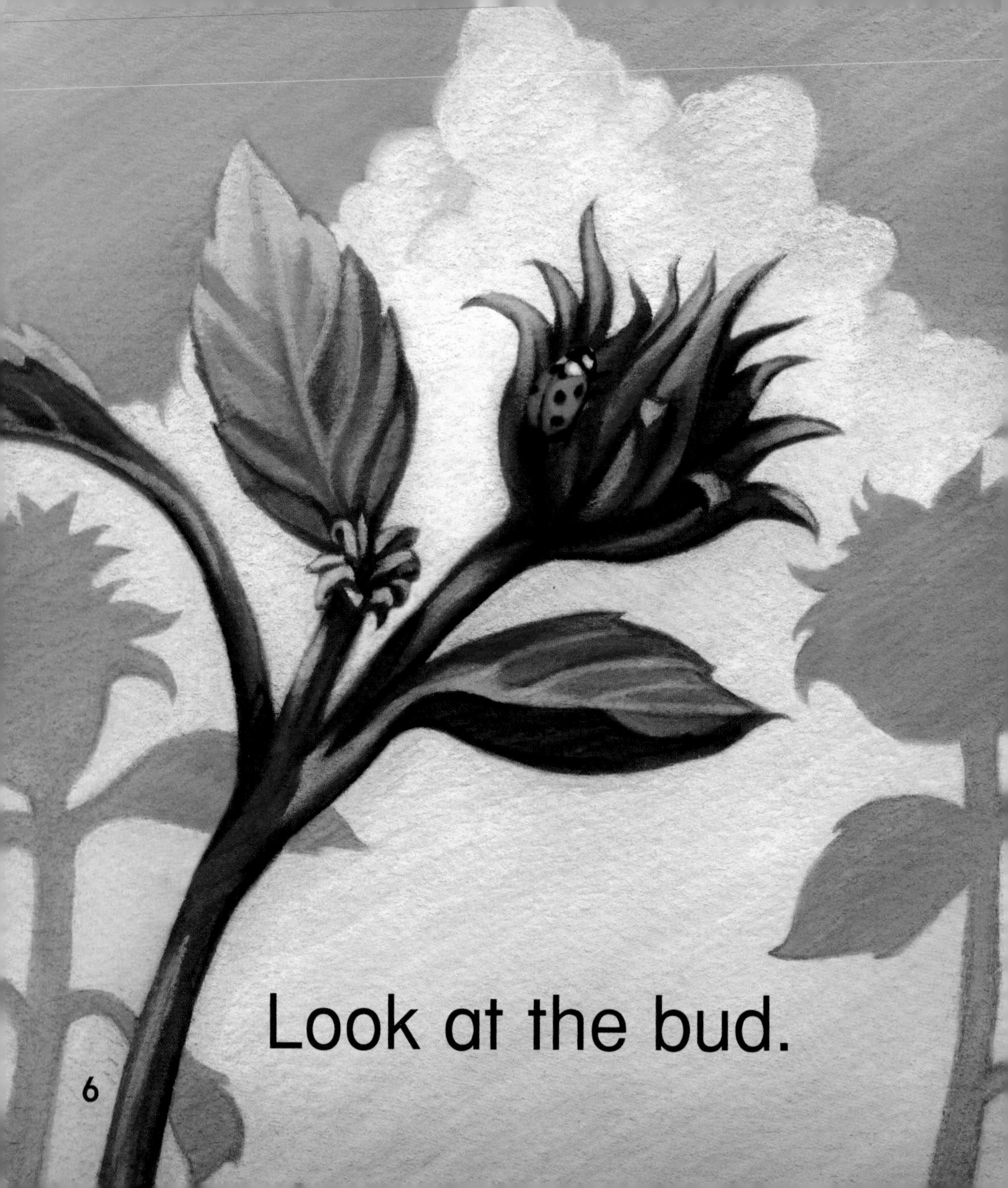

Look at the bud.

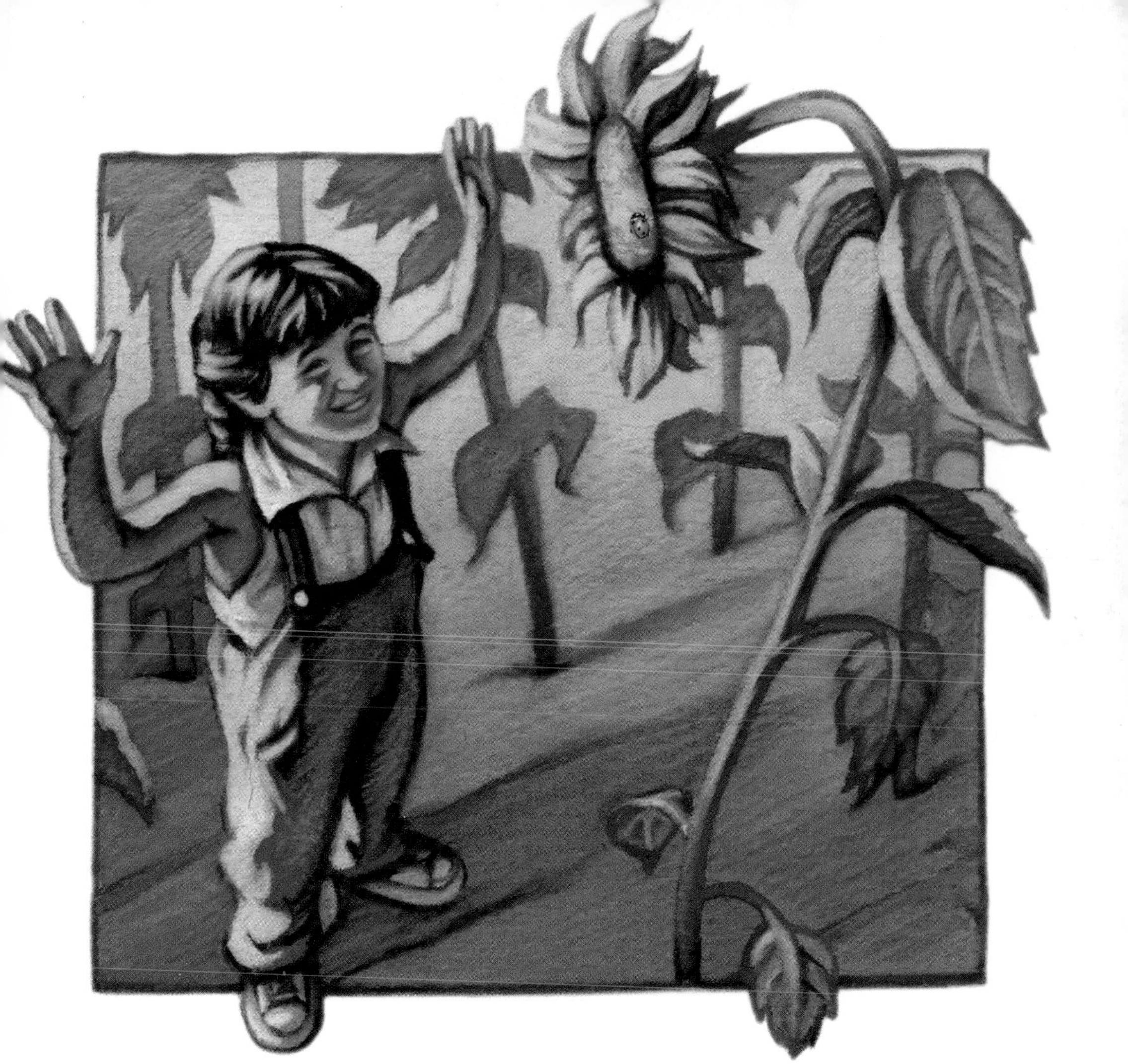

Look at the flower.

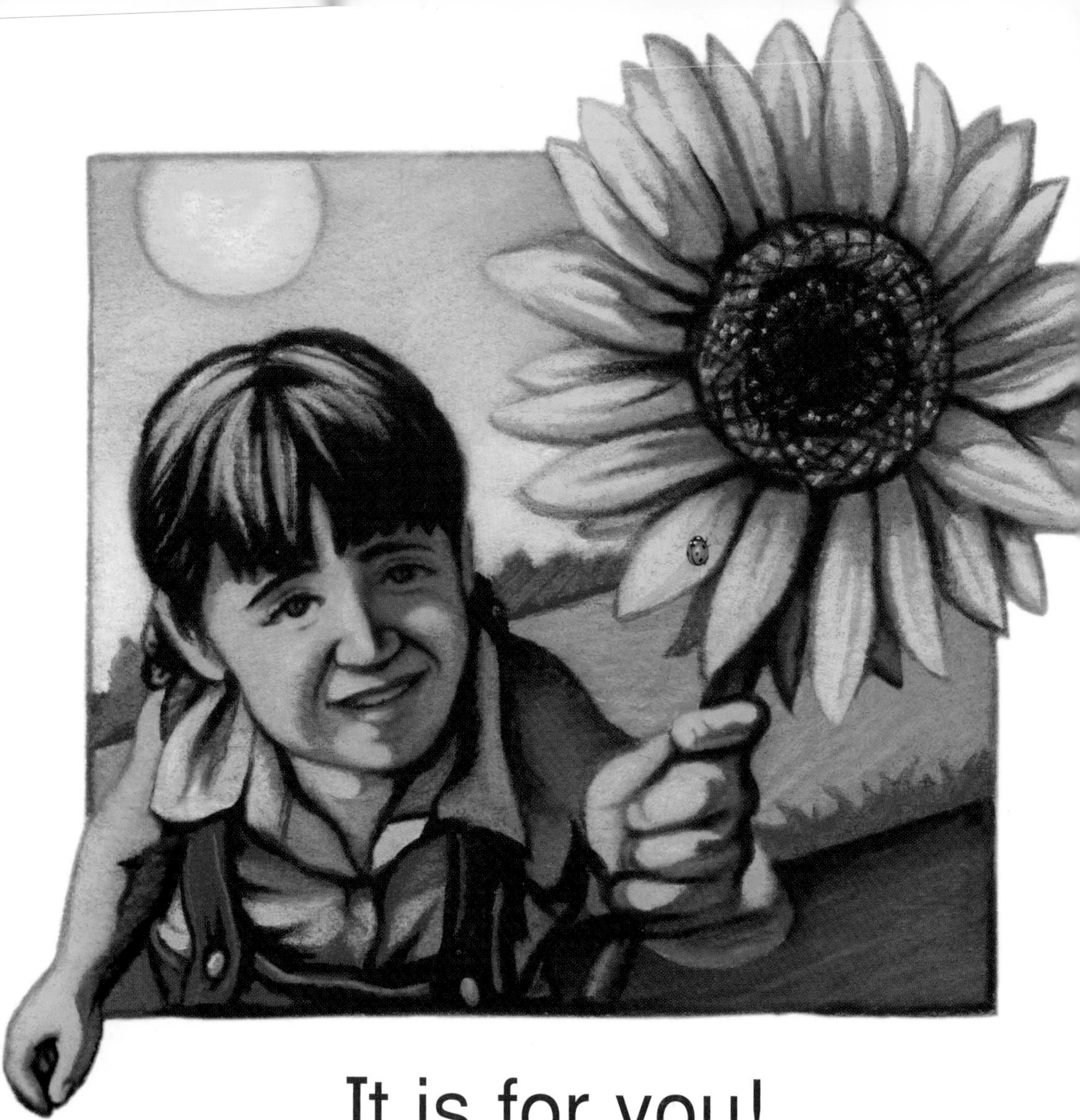

It is for you!